CAREER AS AN
AIR TRAFFIC CONTROLLER

ANYBODY WHO HAS EVER WILED away an hour or two in an airport has spent at least a few minutes wondering how it all works. Enormous aircraft pick up and drop off thousands of passengers all day long, taxiing across runways and aprons on a rigid schedule and doing it so safely that collisions are vanishingly rare. The same aircraft take off and land within minutes of each other, crowding the skies above airports with airborne traffic jams that somehow always manage to keep moving. When they fly thousands of miles to their destinations, pilots almost never make wrong turns. Earthbound highways do not even come close to this level of safety and efficiency.

Air traffic control is one of the professions that keeps the modern world in motion. No longer the province of the wealthy, air travel is now the preferred means to cover long distances, and a vital part of conducting business. The number of passenger miles flown has increased steadily for decades, with more people spending more time in the air every year. Demand for pilots, flight attendants, mechanics and other air travel professionals has increased along with the demand for their services. Demand for air traffic controllers has been especially strong.

Demand goes both ways in the air traffic control career. With a median salary of about $125,000 per year and enviable fringe benefits, many people are competing for jobs as air traffic controllers. About 25,000 people work as air traffic controllers today. Most of them work for the Federal Aviation Administration, or FAA. By federal law, all of them were trained by the FAA even if they went on to work somewhere else. Every year thousands of people take the test to get into the FAA training program, and most of them end up on a list so the FAA can call them when a position opens up in a class. The list is so long that a number of these people find other jobs while they are waiting and never become air traffic controllers.

Take careful note of the information contained in this report. In it you will find sections covering everything from how to prepare for your career as an air traffic controller and what kind of education and training you will need, to what you may like and dislike about the career. If you like what you read here be sure to check out the list of additional resources on the last page of this report. There, you will find even more information to help you learn all you can about a career as an air traffic controller.

WHAT YOU CAN DO NOW

AIR TRAFFIC CONTROL MAY LOOK LIKE A COMPLETE mystery from where you are sitting today. There are ways, however, to learn a thing or two about the career before you really plunge in.

Spend some time around airports. Airports are hard to get into nowadays if you do not have a boarding pass. Many airports, however, cater to flying fans by reserving space near runways for spectators to watch planes as they come and go. Some airports even have picnic areas for onlookers. People have always enjoyed watching planes land and take off, but security concerns caused some airports to restrict the areas near runways. When fans exclaimed that this was unfair, many airports responded by creating formal areas for aircraft watching. Such areas are more comfortable than sitting on the hood of a car hundreds of yards away. They are also easier to patrol by security personnel. Check out airports near you and get to know your fellow fans.

The National Aeronautics and Space Administration – better known as NASA – maintains a great website called Smart Skies that explains the math behind air traffic control. The site offers videos, math problems and even an app to simulate air traffic control. The site has resources for potential careerists who want to learn more about the profession, and for teachers who want to create a special lesson plan for their students.

Finally, there is no better way to learn about the ins and outs of any profession than by reading the professional literature devoted to it. Magazines like *Flying, Plane & Pilot* and *Airliner World* are great sources of information about the world of aviation. The websites of the Federal Aviation Administration (FAA) and the National Air Traffic Controllers Association have great insights into the rules and regulations that air traffic controllers have to deal with every day.

HISTORY OF THE CAREER

PRETTY MUCH EVERYBODY KNOWS that the Wright brothers, Wilbur and Orville, first achieved powered flight with their successful test at Kitty Hawk, North Carolina on December 17, 1903. In four short flights the Wright brothers' rudimentary aircraft, the Flyer, managed to take off under its own power and stay under its pilot's control before landing on a spot equal to or higher than the point from which it took off. Powered flight was born.

Nobody knew what to do with the new invention. The Flyer was a spindly contraption that could barely carry a pilot, let alone passengers or cargo. It took more than a decade for anybody to find commercial uses for flight, and those were for short tourist flights that were mainly for the curious. Aviation technology did not really take off until World War I, when governments on both sides of the Atlantic funded research and development that led to the first high-performance aircraft capable of carrying passengers and cargo. Immediately after the war, however, there were still relatively few planes in the air. What's more, they were all limited to flying during the day because landmarks on the ground provided the only means of navigation.

Early attempts at air traffic control look comical by today's standards. In an effort to create the first airmail service, the United States Postal Service in 1921 used a series of bonfires to guide pilots to their destinations after dark. It sort of worked. By 1923, a series of electric light beacons mounted on towers allowed airmail pilots to cross the United States in about 29 hours, which was several days faster than the trains of the day.

The boom in postal flight inspired Congress to pass the Contract Air Mail Act of 1925, allowing contract carriers to carry mail for the Postal Service, and the Air Commerce Act of 1926, which put the Department of Commerce in charge of establishing rules for flying, pilot training and establishing aids to navigation. The first air traffic controller was hired by the city of St. Louis in 1929. He sat in a wheelbarrow at the edge of the runway and used signal flags to communicate with pilots. Only a year later, Cleveland built the first control center equipped with another new technology: radio. The Department of Commerce had installed 83 radio beacons across the country by 1932, underscoring how important commercial flight was becoming to the country. Air traffic controllers were hired by major airports across the country, but there were still no comprehensive standards in place.

The 1930s brought more advances, including the establishment of the first three air route traffic control centers in Chicago, Cleveland and Newark in 1936, and the creation of the Civil Aeronautics Authority in 1938, put- ting all regulation of the aviation business under federal control. World War II, which the United States entered in 1941, brought enormous changes to the aviation industry, just as World War I had a few decades earlier.

Developed during the war, radar came into common use by the 1950s but was only used to direct approaches and departures at major airports. A midair collision over the Grand Canyon in 1956 that killed all passengers aboard two aircraft led to the creation of the Federal Aviation Agency in 1958. The predecessor to the Federal Aviation Administration made its first mark on aviation safety in 1960 by requiring all aircraft to use radar transponders that allowed them to be tracked by radar. The FAA also standardized training for air traffic controllers and took over operations at major control towers across the country. The FAA used early computer technology to help track aircraft, and by 1975 had deployed a system nationwide that tracked aircraft cross-country and at the 61 busiest airports.

The next big leap in the aviation industry came in 1978, with the passage of the Airline Deregulation Act that allowed airlines to set their own prices for air travel. Competition among airlines quickly brought prices down, resulting in a surge in air traffic. The air traffic control system was not prepared for this surge, resulting in a nationwide strike by air traffic controllers in 1981. Air traffic controllers argued that they were overworked, underpaid and equipped with outdated equipment. Whatever the merits of their claims, more than 11,000 striking controllers were fired when the strike against the federal government was declared illegal. Thousands of flights were cancelled and air traffic control duties were taken over by military personnel, newly trained controllers, and controllers who had escaped the firing. The FAA also temporarily closed many small airports in order to move controllers to the places where they were needed most.

It took the FAA many years to solve the problems that led to the strike. Remember the newfangled computer systems the FAA put into use in the 1960s? They were still in use well into the 1990s. Work rules for air traffic controllers had not changed much, either. Congress passed legislation in 1996 to reform the FAA from the ground up. New technology was deployed and new work rules and pay scales were created that were exclusive to the FAA and separate from the federal government's general schedule that covered most federal employees.

The FAA faced its biggest challenge on September 11, 2001 when terrorists flew hijacked aircraft into the twin towers of the World Trade Center in New York City, the Pentagon in Washington, DC, and a field near Shanksville, Pennsylvania. More than 4,500 aircraft were in the air over the continental United States at the time of the attacks. All of them were safely on the ground in less than three hours. For the first time in history, the airspace over the United States was completely closed.

Today air traffic controllers work in more than 350 airports and 21 Air Route Traffic Control Centers across the United States. Surprisingly, there is no specific criterion for which airports have air traffic controllers and which do not. About 15,000 small airports in the United States do not have air traffic controllers and many airports that do have them do not operate 24 hours a day. Airports generally receive towers and controllers when local authorities make the case that traffic has increased to the point where air traffic control has become necessary to ensure safety. If the FAA agrees with the assessment, it will fund construction of a tower and pay the salaries of controllers. Sometimes cities or private companies build towers and hire controllers themselves. This is perfectly legal as long as controllers, towers and equipment are all FAA-certified. About 10 percent of all air traffic controllers in the United States are employed by organizations other than the FAA.

WHERE YOU WILL WORK

AIR TRAFFIC CONTROLLERS CAN BE FOUND anywhere there is an airport big enough to warrant a control tower. Not all airports do. Most small airports intended for use by private planes do not have control towers or air traffic controllers because there is not enough traffic to warrant them. Any airport big enough to attract significant numbers of corporate or charter aircraft will have a control tower and a few air traffic controllers.

In order to become air traffic controllers careerists have to agree to go wherever the FAA needs them. After you have passed all the tests to become an air traffic controller, the FAA will put you where it needs you for the first two to four years of your career. During these years you will be a developmental controller, or an apprentice of sorts. Once you make the grade and drop the "developmental" from your title you can apply for openings anywhere you want. It stands to reason that there will be more openings in busy metropolitan areas like Chicago or New York, but it should also come as no surprise that many careerists would like to work in those cities. There is no magic formula for spending your career exactly where you want. If you want to go to Los Angeles, there will be more opportunities but also more competition. If you have your heart set on a job in Lincoln, Nebraska you probably will not face as much competition but you could wait a long time for a position to open up.

The United States military owns and staffs many air traffic control towers all over the world. In fact, many air traffic controllers get their start in the military. The Air Force and Navy employ the most air traffic controllers by far, followed by the Marine Corps, Coast Guard and the Army. Military air traffic controllers are employed in control towers at bases across the United States and around the world. Military air traffic controllers are often called upon to take over control towers in combat zones if the tower has been abandoned. They can also be called in to take over operations at a tower that has been captured from the enemy so that the airfield can be used by American and allied aircraft. The Navy trains air traffic controllers two ways: for airports on land and for flight operations onboard aircraft carriers. If you choose to start your career in the military, you could find yourself directing traffic in some very interesting places.

DESCRIPTION OF WORK DUTIES

Tower Controllers

Tower controllers are the first air traffic controllers to take charge of aircraft. They are responsible for directing traffic on the ground and in the air. Their purview includes not just aircraft, but also everything on the tarmac at an airport, from aircraft to luggage trolleys to emergency vehicles to those portable stairs that can be driven around and attached to planes on the ground for boarding and deplaning. They manage air traffic and ground traffic.

Tower controllers are primarily concerned with directing aircraft from three to 30 miles out, and around runways, taxiways and aprons. These are the areas that together are typically referred to as the tarmac, which is the name for the type of asphalt used for airports. Aircraft take off and land on runways, drive to runways on taxiways and park on aprons. It is easy to learn more about how airports are laid out. Get on the internet and look up satellite photos of airports. You will be able to see quite clearly how airports are laid out to ensure the smooth flow of traffic.

Aircraft tend to evolve more quickly than airports. Most airports are owned by cities and are constructed according to city contracts often funded by special taxing districts. These planning processes do not move as quickly as the aerospace industry, which is one of the most innovative industries in the world. When the Boeing 747 debuted for commercial use in 1970, it rendered many airports obsolete because it was so big that it could not fit on crowded taxiways and aprons. Most major airports needed many years to adapt to the new jumbo jet. The Airbus A380 challenged airports yet again when it came into service in 2007. The A380 is so big that it can only fly into a few dozen airports in the whole world. One A380 on the tarmac can be a major challenge in a tower controller's day.

Tower controllers also give aircraft clearance to take off and land, which is a critical part of the air traffic control process. They have to check flights plans before aircraft take off and make sure enough time has elapsed between takeoffs to ensure relatively calm air for each plane. Big planes leave enormous turbulence behind them, while small planes leave relatively little. This is just one of the many details tower controllers need to know to do their job.

In busy areas tower controllers hand off their aircraft to approach and departure controllers to get them safely out of congested airspace.

Approach and Departure Controllers

Approach and departure controllers mostly work in terminal radar approach control centers, usually known by the acronym TRACONs. TRACONs are located in major metropolitan areas where air traffic is heaviest, and they may be responsible for air traffic originating from more than one airport.

For incoming flights, approach and departure controllers take over from their enroute colleagues about 20 miles from the airport and make sure that aircraft have enough space between them to land safely. The distance is approximate as aircraft originating from multiple airports may travel different distances before they are handed off. Some overlap between different types of controllers is intentional and necessary to make sure that every aircraft is accounted for and that controllers make enough room for all of them to fly safely. Commercial aircraft travel at hundreds of miles per hour, leaving very little time to take evasive action if something goes wrong with a plane coming in for a landing. Trailing aircraft need to have enough time to change course if a problem develops with the plane in front of them. Approach and departure controllers also tell pilots about the local weather and anything else they need to know as they approach the airport.

Approach and departure controllers take over outgoing aircraft from tower controllers at the edge of their range, also usually about 20 miles from the airport. They control the aircraft until it is about 50 miles from the airport and assist pilots to safely climb out of the congestion around the airport and onto their flight path. Then they pass them off to enroute controllers.

Enroute Controllers

Enroute controllers work in one of 24 air route traffic control centers across the United States and are responsible for controlling aircraft for most of a typical flight. Enroute controllers track aircraft from the moment they leave the TRACON airspace until the moment they depart the airspace controlled by their air route traffic control center. Then they make sure the aircraft are handed off to enroute controllers in the next area of responsibility, or to approach and departure controllers if they are nearing their destination.

Air route traffic control centers are not located at or even very near airports, so they tend to be overlooked by the flying public. Although their work does not seem quite as dramatic as the work of approach and departure controllers and tower controllers, enroute controllers keep air traffic moving smoothly from coast to coast. They tell pilots to change their altitude or slightly adjust their heading in order to make sure everybody has enough sky to fly through safely. Ask pilots and they will tell you that their goal is to fly through the middle of the air, away from the ground on the one side and space on the other. Enroute controllers keep pilots in the middle of the air where they belong.

Enroute controllers are also usually the first to notice when aircraft deviate from their flight plans, indicating that something is wrong. You might be surprised how often private pilots become unconscious or die while in flight, due to health issues or problems with the pressurization systems in their planes. Their planes just fly until they run out of fuel and crash.

Supervisory Air Traffic Control Specialists

After many years on the job, some air traffic controllers decide that they want to enter administrative positions. As supervisory air traffic control specialists, they no longer perform hands-on air traffic control but take over the day-to-day management of their fellow controllers. They manage training and development programs, pass along their accumulated knowledge to new controllers and take care of ordinary managerial tasks like scheduling and approving vacation plans.

Like most managers, supervisory air traffic control specialists are paid more than their colleagues without leadership responsibilities. They may also get to work more hours that are regular and have more control over their schedules. The downside is that they will spend less time controlling aircraft.

AIR TRAFFIC CONTROLLERS TELL THEIR STORIES

I Am a Tower Controller at a Major Airport

"My job is crazy. Hundreds of aircraft come through my airport every day, at all hours. Thousands of passengers and crew members come with them, along with thousands more airport employees, many of whom work on the tarmac and contribute to the traffic my colleagues and I are responsible for controlling. The margin for error is essentially zero. That's crazy.

I earned a two-year AT-CTI degree after high school and scored above 85 on the FAA exam, which put me at the top of the list for a spot in an FAA Academy class. It still took a little more than a year to get the call. I accepted of course.

I became fully certified after four years as a developmental controller. I spent those years at a medium-sized airport, which was an excellent place to learn the trade. It was just busy enough to create plenty of opportunities for learning but not as crazy as my current job.

Tower controllers have to keep track of everything on the tarmac, and that's a lot! There are luggage trolleys and maintenance vehicles, passenger and crew shuttles, those drivable stairs, emergency vehicles and even the occasional lost dog. Most people don't think about these things when they think of air traffic controllers, but we're the first step in the process. One of the most important things we have to think about is "max on ground," or MOG. That's the number of aircraft our tarmac can safely accommodate at one time. A typical shopping mall has more parking space than most airports. If airport operations are backed up we have to tell pilots to circle or even land at alternate airports because we have nowhere for them to park. Thousands of aircraft were diverted to different airports on September 11, 2001 not just because we wanted to get them out of the sky for security reasons, but because we had to find places for them to park. The system assumes that a large percentage of aircraft will be in the air at all times. If they all landed at once, the system would get bogged down and we would have a very big mess to straighten out.

Tower controllers also give pilots final clearance to take off and land. For takeoff, we guide them through the traffic on the ground and send them on their way. For landing, we make sure they have enough room, give them a slot and guide them to their gate or other parking place on the tarmac."

I Am an Approach and Departure Controller

"I work in a TRACON (Terminal Radar Approach Control) on the edge of a major metropolitan area, just where the air traffic starts to thicken up. My job is to make sure that aircraft coming into the airports in my area have enough room to climb and land safely. This is where we start to line everybody up.

Look at a map of flight routes across the United States and you'll see that the routes start to converge about 50 miles out from major metropolitan areas. There's plenty of room way out west, for example, and enroute controllers make sure that everybody stays on course. But get into the general vicinity of a densely populated area and all those lines start to converge. Search the internet for flight plans on a site like iFlightPlanner or on an airline website showing their routes and you'll see what I mean. That's why there are three distinct sets of air traffic controllers. Tower controllers to manage airport traffic, approach and departure controllers to manage traffic near airports and enroute controllers to keep everything orderly in-between. On a cross-country flight from Los Angeles to Baltimore, for example, a pilot may talk to 28 different controllers in 11 different facilities.

Like many air traffic controllers, I got my start in the military. One five-year hitch in the Air Force gave me the start I needed to succeed at the FAA Academy and slide into this civilian career. I wouldn't trade my military experience for anything. Once, I was on a team of controllers who took over a control tower in a war zone after it had been captured by American forces. We got it up and running in less than a day so we could use the airport to move people and supplies in and out of the area. It was a very impressive operation.

This job is a lot like being a police officer. Most of the time, being a cop is pretty easy. You go on patrol, you do your job, you go home at the end of your shift and all is well. Then there are those days when everything that can go wrong does go wrong. There is no time to get angry or frustrated. Your pleasant daily routine blows up in a matter of seconds and everybody looks to you to make it right. People you've never met are depending upon you and you need to make high-stakes decisions right away. That's what it's like to be an air traffic controller. You have to be ready every day for any eventuality."

I Am an Air Traffic Controller for the United States Navy

"My job is very cool. As an air traffic controller for the US Navy, I have worked in air traffic control facilities at Navy bases in the United States, several foreign countries and aboard two aircraft carriers. Nobody else in this line of work has the kind of opportunities I do. I wouldn't trade it for anything.

If you'd asked me in high school what I wanted my life to be like, I would have said that I wanted it to be an adventure. I was never very clear on how I was going to achieve this adventure mind you, but anything less than 24-hour-a-day excitement just wasn't going to cut it. I could not understand how my friends could get excited about becoming lawyers or accountants or whatever. No matter how they described those careers they all sounded like desk jobs to me. Not my thing.

I joined the Navy almost on a whim. I had been out of high school for a couple of years, worked a few jobs I didn't like very much, took a couple of college classes and generally drifted around and hoped I would stumble across something that got me excited. I wasn't desperate, I was just bored.

A Navy recruiter caught me looking at a poster outside a recruiting station. I hadn't gone to the recruiting station – it just happened to be next-door to a sandwich shop where I went for lunch. We started chatting. He showed me brochures about career opportunities in the Navy, explained how I could earn the GI Bill to pay for college and the VA Loan to pay for a house with just one five-year hitch. What finally sold me was the opportunity to see the world. That sounded like the adventure I needed.

It took some haggling but eventually we settled on the air traffic controller rating, or AC. I didn't know this at first, but when you join the military you don't have to sign anything until you have a contract for a job you actually want. I wanted to be an AC. I signed the paperwork, shipped off to boot camp, went from there to the 16-week AC school and then 'out to the fleet.'

In my case, that meant to a naval air station in Virginia, where I worked as a developmental tower controller under senior controllers. It took me three years to become fully certified, after which I moved to my favorite posting: an aircraft carrier.

There are only about 14 full-fledged aircraft carriers in the entire world. Britain, France and Russia each has one. The rest are all American. Each of our carriers sails with roughly 85 aircraft, including transport aircraft, airborne early warning aircraft, fighter planes and helicopters. They fly from a flight deck about five acres in size. That seems big right up until you see it from the primary flight control center, just above the bridge on the island superstructure. That's when you notice it's so crowded that aircraft parked around the edge of the flight deck actually hang over the side to make as much room for flight operations as possible.

I work for the air boss and the mini boss, the two people in charge of air traffic control. My job is to stay in contact with pilots as they approach and depart the carrier to make sure that there is adequate time between sorties – individual flights – and that incoming aircraft don't approach until aircraft that have just landed have cleared the flight deck. I keep waiting aircraft in what we call a "Marshall Stack" above the carrier, which is a stack of aircraft circling the carrier and waiting their turn to land. The name comes from a brand of guitar amplifier used by heavy metal musicians!

I have been in the Navy for 10 years now and recently signed up for my third five-year enlistment. I have been taking college classes and am working toward an AT-CTI-certified degree so that I can continue my career after I retire. I joined the Navy at 20 years old and can retire with a pension after 20 years of service. My plan is to join the FAA after I get out and continue my career. With my Navy experience and an AT-CTI degree I will land at the top of the list for FAA jobs. That's a pretty good plan if I do say so myself."

I Am an Enroute Controller

"I get no glory, and I like it that way. As an enroute air traffic controller, I guide aircraft through wide-open spaces in-between airports. I don't work in a tower that can be seen for miles and my airspace almost never sees congestion like that around airports. But if I didn't do my job here in my air route traffic control center the skies would be a lot more dangerous.

My airspace is very large and is right smack in the middle of the continental United States. There are a few cities near my airspace, like St. Louis and Kansas City, but I am nowhere near Los Angeles or Chicago. My airspace doesn't have to deal with dense concentrations of aircraft, but we do have to deal with essentially all aircraft flying cross country.

When aircraft enter our space, they are either at cruising altitude or are still climbing from one of the airports near our area. Cruising altitude can mean a lot of things. For a small private plane cruising altitude can be anywhere from 2,500 feet to 10,000 feet. Commercial aircraft fly at more like 35,000 feet, and military aircraft can fly higher than that. Keeping everybody in their lane requires thinking in three dimensions. Two cars traveling in the same lane at the same speed can easily collide because they are always at the same level. Two aircraft can be on the same flight path at the same speed and still be miles away from each other because they fly at different altitudes. My one and only job, when you get right down to it, is making sure everybody has enough room to fly safely.

You might not think it, but enroute controllers see our fair share of drama. We are usually the first to know when something goes wrong aboard an aircraft because we see the planes depart from their flight plans. Enroute controllers were the first to notice that the four planes used in the September 11th terrorist attacks departed from their flight plans. It's also enroute controllers who usually track plane crashes. Small planes crash in alarming numbers, but you rarely hear about it because only one or two people were aboard them."

PERSONAL QUALITIES

NOT EVERYONE IS CUT OUT TO BE AN AIR TRAFFIC controller. To be successful in this profession you should be rock-steady under pressure, and able to make complex decisions on the fly.

Air traffic control is a famously stressful profession. The sheer magnitude of what is at stake each and every day is immense and has very few parallels in other professions. This reality has manifested itself in movies about air traffic controllers working feverishly to manage an in-flight emergency, innumerable jokes about stress in the control tower, and funny lines exchanged between pilots and controllers. The movies may be overly dramatized and the jokes share the kind of black humor also used by soldiers and police officers, but there is more than a little truth to them. To be a successful air traffic controller you have to be able to control your emotions when things get complicated. Becoming overcome with fear and indecision can lead to disaster. You need to be able to see past your emotional response to an emergency and keep your wits about you. Most people are not very good at this. If you cannot stand pressure, if you do not want to make life-and-death decisions with regularity, this is not the career for you.

Air traffic controllers need to be able to keep their wits about them in emergencies because pilots and ground crews depend upon them to make the critical decisions that will keep a problem from becoming a disaster. This can get complicated. You may be able to remain level-headed under immense pressure, but how well do you know your job? Air traffic controllers do not have time to look up regulations or search the internet to find out what somebody else did when faced with a similar problem. They have to know. Right now. This kind of analytical skill is critical to success in this profession. Even for routine operations, when everything is going smoothly, air traffic controllers have to be in nonstop problem-solving mode. Pilots will always have questions and they will always need reliable answers.

This is why air traffic controllers need to have unassailable communications skills. Like police officers, air traffic controllers learn a professional vocabulary that is supposed to cover most situations. In practice, however, code words and official phrases are never enough. Air traffic controllers need to be able to communicate whatever a pilot needs to know, quickly, clearly and with no ambiguity whatsoever. This goes both ways, too. Air traffic controllers need to be able to listen carefully to pilots and not hesitate to ask questions if they are not sure they understand something. Crystal-clear communication is essential in this career. Also, English is the official language of air traffic control in the United States (and in most of the rest of the world).

ATTRACTIVE FEATURES

IT IS NO WONDER SO MANY PEOPLE want to be air traffic controllers. For starters, the job pays extremely well and job security is also excellent.

The median annual salary for air traffic controllers is about $130,000 per year. That is more than twice the average household income in the United States. Unlike other federal employees, air traffic controllers are not paid according to the General Schedule, the pay system that covers most federal employees. The pay scale for air traffic controllers is much higher than for other federal employees with similar experience. There are good reasons for this, of course. Air traffic control is an incredibly difficult job. The margin for error is essentially zero, and air traffic controllers have to live with multiple requirements that most federal employees do not, including minimum health standards. Nobody will ever tell you this is an easy job, but air traffic controllers are paid well to do it.

It is hard to beat federal government jobs for job security. Demand never wavers. Your job always needs to be done. The government does not have good years and bad years like a business. Everybody gets paid on time, every time. The only time air traffic controllers have been shown the door was in 1981 when President Ronald Reagan fired more than 11,000 of them when they refused to return to work during a strike.

Air traffic controllers also receive excellent benefits, including healthcare, paid time off, retirement pensions, childcare, and many other perks. Nobody ever got rich as an air traffic controller because there are no opportunities for entrepreneurship. On the other hand, the level of employment is very high.

Maybe most importantly, being an air traffic controller is an excellent way to get a front-row seat to much of the action that makes the world go 'round. Airports are incredibly important to the functioning of the global economy. It is easy to see the importance of the business conducted at each end of a flight – people do not fly for the sake of flying, they fly in order to go places and accomplish things – but it is easy to overlook the business done in-between. The air-travel industry is a multibillion-dollar business that literally spans the globe. As an air traffic controller, you will be right in the heart of the action.

UNATTRACTIVE ASPECTS

AIR TRAFFIC CONTROL IS ONE OF THE MOST stressful jobs imaginable. Stress is a huge part of the daily life of an air traffic controller. An air traffic controller working at a major metropolitan airport is responsible for the safety of hundreds of aircraft and thousands of passengers, flight crew and ground crew. All of these people and machines are in constant motion. Aircraft land and take off from the same runways, many of which intersect each other. Outbound aircraft take to skies filled with inbound aircraft waiting their turn to land. On the ground, enormous aircraft have to maneuver amongst hundreds of obstacles ranging from other aircraft, to luggage trolleys, to emergency vehicles and personnel working on the tarmac. There are tanks of highly flammable fuel everywhere. Heavy rain or high winds make everything worse. Even small mistakes could have deadly consequences. The FAA imposes regulations that try to take the edge off the stress, like enforced rest periods between shifts and a mandatory retirement age of 56, but nothing can put air traffic controllers entirely at ease. If you want to be an air traffic controller, you need to be able to eat stress for breakfast.

If the overwhelming responsibility is not enough to make you think twice, the screwy schedules add another wrinkle to the equation. Air traffic control is classic shift work. Somebody has to be on duty all the time. Major airports are 24-hour operations, and there is absolutely no lull for controllers working in the 24 air route traffic control centers across the United States. If you pursue this career you will have to work many overnight shifts, weekend shifts and other less-than-ideal times like holidays, until you accrue some seniority and can request better hours. Controllers working at small airports may work pretty regular daytime hours, but working at a small airport comes with tradeoffs, like living in a small metropolitan area and having fewer opportunities to move up the ladder. If you pursue a career in a major metropolitan area with a busy airport you will spend many nights, weekends and holidays away from home.

Do you still want to pursue a career as an air traffic controller? Study for the test, score a 70 or higher – and preferably an 85 or higher – and get onto the list. Then wait. It could be a long time until you get the call, during which time you will have to make a living. What will you do? You must get the call before you turn 30 or you will become ineligible to start the FAA training.

EDUCATION AND TRAINING

THE ONLY WAY TO BECOME AN AIR TRAFFIC CONTROLLER is to become certified by the Federal Aviation Administration. You can do this by graduating from the FAA Academy or by gaining certification though military service. There are several ways to set yourself up for success. Whichever one you choose, you are required by law to start the FAA training before you reach your 31st birthday. This is not a good career choice for late-in-life career changers.

No matter which route you take you will have to pass the Air Traffic Standard Aptitude Test, or AT-SAT, a standardized test required of all FAA Academy applicants, except military veterans who are already certified. A score of 70 means you are qualified for FAA training and is enough to get your name onto the list of applicants to be called for a seat in an FAA Academy class. A score of 85 or above means you are well qualified. Well-qualified applicants get called first. The test takes eight hours and aims to evaluate your ability to become an air traffic controller. Study guides are available.

The first way to start on the path to FAA certification is to prove that you are a responsible adult by completing at least three years of progressively responsible work experience, four years of college or some combination of the two. Your work experience does not have to be related to the aviation industry and you do not necessarily have to earn a degree – although both definitely work in an applicant's favor – but you do have to prove that you are a responsible professional. All applicants to the FAA Academy have to be US citizens, pass a medical evaluation and background check, be fluent in English and pass the FAA pre-employment test that includes a biographical assessment. Jump through all of these hoops, pass the test and you may qualify for the 12-week program at the FAA Academy in Oklahoma City, Okla.

The most straightforward way to get started on a career in air traffic control is to graduate from an accredited Air Traffic Collegiate Training Initiative (AT-CTI) program. Many schools offer AT-CTI programs in both two-year associate degree and four-year bachelor's degree formats. The basic curriculum for the associate degree covers such topics as meteorology, aviation safety, aviation history, air traffic control regulations, aviation technology and basic navigation. Students pursuing the bachelor's degree will also tackle topics like airport management, airline infrastructure, aviation law and air traffic management. Graduates of an approved AT-CTI program get to skip the first five weeks of the 12-week FAA Academy program. It will also be easier to pass the test after completing the training program.

The associate degree is enough to get you in the door and get started on your career. The bachelor's degree program will help you to move through the ranks faster. No matter which program you choose, you should complete an internship. Most FAA internships are unpaid and are offered as part of the Volunteer Service Program. The FAA sometimes offers a very limited number of paid internships consisting of hands-on work experience, although the program is not offered ever year due to budgetary constraints. Internships give aspiring careerists valuable work experience while they are still in school and save the FAA money by using students as relatively inexpensive assistants to working air traffic controllers. The best interns move to the top of the FAA's waiting list for available positions. Be sure to take advantage of this opportunity.

The final way to become FAA-certified is to learn your trade in the military. All of the armed services use air traffic controllers. The Navy and Air Force employ the most, followed by the Marine Corps, Coast Guard and Army. All of the services train their own air traffic controllers, and the FAA accredits all service schools. It should come as no surprise that many air traffic controllers started their careers in the military. Training comes with the job and the job comes with adventures you will never get if you work in the same control tower for your entire career. Military service also comes with benefits like the GI Bill, which can pay for college, and the VA Loan, which can help you to buy a home. Not everybody who joins the military makes a long-term career out of it, but one five-year hitch is an excellent way to get started in life.

Never forget that there are typically many more applicants than there are jobs available. Your best bets to get into this profession are to earn an AT-CTI-accredited degree, become certified in the military or pass the AT-SAT with a score of 85 or better. Some combination of these options would be best of all.

EARNINGS

LIKE JOBS WITH MOST FEDERAL AGENCIES, jobs with the FAA pay well and come with excellent benefits. The military pays well too and comes with its own benefits. The few other organizations that employ air traffic controllers tend to come with similar pay and benefits, but there is no standardized pay scale for private employers. Also, the only way you can become an air traffic controller with a private company is by getting certified by the FAA, which requires spending a few years working for the FAA first. Since you are just starting out on your career you need to set your sights on an FAA job. If you want to work for a private company, you can make that decision later in your career.

About 90 percent of the 24,000 or so air traffic controllers working in the United States work for the FAA. While the average salary for an FAA air traffic controller is about $130,000 per year, the reality is a bit complicated. For starters, the FAA is one of the few federal agencies that does not use the General Schedule for its employees. The General Schedule sets the salaries for all but the highest-ranking federal employees. The FAA pays its employees according to one of six specialized pay plans. The Air Traffic Compensation Plan covers air traffic control specialists, traffic management coordinators and specialists, air traffic managers, supervisors, operations and support employees, flight service specialists and related staff. All FAA pay is subject to locality differences, meaning that a controller based in an expensive city like New York will be paid more than a controller based in an inexpensive city like Memphis. Many small markets do not get locality pay, and are paid the same basic pay. The basic pay for air traffic control specialists starts at about $40,000 per year for what is called "arrival guarantee," or pay for training while at the FAA Academy. Pay increases for developmental controllers as they achieve proficiency and reach D1, D2 and D3 status, signifying 25-percent, 50-percent and 75-percent completion of training. Pay for D1 controllers, for example, starts at about $47,000 per year. Basic pay for D2 controllers starts at just over $50,000, and D3 starts at about $58,00 per year.

Certified controllers earn a minimum of $64,000 per year, while the basic pay is almost $150,000 per year. If you look up these numbers on the FAA website – and you should – please keep in mind that different controllers are offered different pay scales based upon their incoming qualifications and performance on the job. The locality differences can be quite significant, too. The top of the pay scale for controllers stationed in San Diego, California, a very expensive place to live, is almost $190,000 per year.

Military pay is governed by a rank-based pay scale that starts at E-1, for new enlisted personnel attending boot camp, to O-10, for four-star admirals and generals (of which there are very few!). Air traffic controllers in the military can be found in both the officer and enlisted ranks, depending upon the needs of each service and the specific career path chosen by each careerist. Military pay ranges from $1,500 per month for new enlisted recruits, to over $15,000 per month for four-star admirals and generals. You can expect to spend most of your career somewhere in-between these extremes. Keep in mind that military compensation also comes with a housing allowance, special pay for deploying to combat zones and other bonuses depending upon your contract. Military personnel sometimes get free meals, too! Military pay tables are available on the Defense Finance and Accounting Service website.

OPPORTUNITIES

ALTHOUGH YOU CAN SET YOURSELF UP FOR SUCCESS as an air traffic controller in several different ways, there is really only one path to landing a job. Networking and making the right friends will do you no good in this business. You have to follow the same path everybody else does.

All federal jobs are advertised on the USAJOBS. To start the long process of becoming an air traffic controller you need to wait for a job announcement. You will have to fill out the application, which is quite lengthy. Do not leave anything out and be sure to be scrupulously honest. You will be subjected to a background investigation later in the process and the investigators are very thorough. One to two months after the application period closes you will be invited to take the AT-SAT (unless there are more applicants than there are testing slots, in which case applicants will be chosen at random). Take the test and aim for an 85 or better. Of note, each job announcement has specific requirements. If you have military experience, for example, and apply for a position specifically offered to veterans, your training and certification requirements will be different than those for civilian applicants with no prior experience. If you have prior experience and apply for a job open to the general public you may have to complete all of the requirements despite your experience.

It could be a long time before you get the call but when you do, you will start the process by sitting for an interview. Military veterans and graduates of accredited AT-CTI programs qualify for an expedited process. Then you will have to fill out a federal form SF-86, which is used for the background investigation for your security clearance. You will have to line up friends and professional associates to sit for interviews with investigators and be prepared for an exhaustive interview yourself. This process could take a year.

Then you will get to take the Minnesota Multiphasic Personality Inventory to make sure you have the right personality for such a stressful job.

If you are still in the running, you will next be required to pass a physical exam and a drug screening. Nobody expects deskbound air traffic controllers to be able to do hundreds of pushups. The physical screening is to make sure you are healthy and are not likely to faint when things get hectic. Finally, you will get to do an interview with an FAA representative. If you pass, you will receive a letter offering you a job.

The paychecks will not start yet. You will still have to wait for an offer for a seat in an FAA Academy class. Then you have to complete the class. After that, you are off to your first assignment as a developmental air traffic controller. Most new careerists become certified within two to four years. Those with prior experience, such as military experience, usually become certified much faster. Keep this in mind as you consider your options for entering this career.

GETTING STARTED

THERE ARE MANY CHALLENGES BETWEEN YOU AND your dream career as an air traffic controller. Competition may be keen but so is demand. Demand for air traffic controllers is expected to rise somewhat more slowly than for many other professions, but that rise is also expected to be consistent for the foreseeable future. Most air traffic controllers serve until they turn 56 and are required to retire. There is not much turnover before that age. As air travel gets less expensive demand keeps going up. Hiring tends to pop in specific places as airports expand to meet demand.

Expanding an airport can be a very costly, time-consuming process but when the time comes to hire new controllers you need to be ready.

Even if you think you want to earn a degree from an accredited AT-CTI program at a college or university, do not ignore the military option. One five-year hitch in any of the five military services can get you FAA certification and the kind of real-world experience you will not get anywhere else. Military air traffic controllers are in high demand by the FAA, and it should be easy to see why. The FAA knows that applicants with military experience have a good work ethic and have already faced many stressful situations on the job. There is no substitute for this kind of experience. You will also become eligible for the GI Bill, which could pay for an aviation-related degree of your choice.

Do not worry too much about your first posting as a developmental controller. As soon as you become certified you can put in for a transfer to a new location. It may take a while to get to where you want to be, but you will have plenty of opportunities to learn and grow as a professional along the way. Keep an open mind and you will do just fine. Good luck!

ASSOCIATIONS, PERIODICALS, WEBSITES

■ **Airbus**
www.airbus.com

■ **Airliner World**
www.airlinerworld.com

- **Airport Ground Transportation Association**
www.agtaweb.org

- **Airports Council International – North America**
www.aci-na.org

- **Air Traffic Control Association**
www.atca.org

- **Airways Magazine**
www.airwaysmag.com

- **American Association of Airport Executives**
www.aaae.org

- **Boeing**
www.boeing.com

- **Bombardier**
www.bombardier.com

- **Dassault Aviation**
www.dassault-aviation.com

- **Defense Finance and Accounting Service**
www.dfas.mil

- **Embry-Riddle Aeronautical University**
www.erau.edu

- **Federal Aviation Administration**
www.faa.gov

- **Flight Stats**
www.flightstats.com

- **Flying Magazine**
www.flyingmag.com

- **iFlightPlanner**
www.iflightplanner.com

- **International Air Transport Association**
www.iata.org

- **International Civil Aviation Organization**
www.icao.int

- **Lewis University**
www.lewisu.edu

- **Middle Tennessee State University**
www.mtsu.edu

- **Midwest ATC**
www.atctower.com

- **Minnesota State University, Mankato**
www.mankato.mnsu.edu

- **National Air Traffic Controllers Association**
www.natca.org

- **National Business Aviation Association**
www.nbaa.org

- **National Geospatial-Intelligence Agency**
www.nga.mil

- **Plane and Pilot**
www.planeandpilotmag.com

- **Purdue University**
www.purdue.edu

- **Robinson Aviation**
www.rvainc.com

- **Routes Online**
  www.routesonline.com

- **San Jose State University**
  www.sjsu.edu

- **Serco Services**
  www.serco-na.com

- **Smart Skies**
  www.smartskies.nasa.gov

- **Southern Illinois University**
  www.siu.edu

- **United States Air Force**
  www.airforce.com

- **United States Army**
  www.goarmy.com

- **United States Coast Guard**
  www.gocoastguard.com

- **United States Marine Corps**
  www.marines.com

- **United States Navy**
  www.navy.com

- **USA JOBS**
  www.usajobs.com

- **University of Alaska Anchorage**
  www.uaa.alaska.edu

- **Vaughn College**
  www.vaughn.edu

Copyright 2019
Institute For Career Research
CAREERS INTERNET DATABASE

www.careers-internet.org

Made in the USA
Columbia, SC
29 December 2023